TINY BUDDHA'S
Worry Journal

TINY BUDDHA'S
Worry Journal

A Creative Way to Let Go of Anxiety
and Find Peace

LORI DESCHENE

Coloring Pages by Rose Hwang

HarperOne
An Imprint of HarperCollinsPublishers

HarperOne

All coloring page artwork by Rose Hwang.

HarperCollins books may be purchased for educational, business, or sales promotional use. For information, please email the Special Markets Department at SPsales@harpercollins.com.

FIRST EDITION

Designed by Yvonne Chan
Cloud illustration by maritime_m/Shutterstock

ISBN 978-0-06-284987-8

19 20 21 22   LSC   10 9 8 7 6 5

INTRODUCTION

Worry and anxiety—two issues we've all struggled with to some degree. While they often go hand in hand, they're two distinct psychological states. Whether you're obsessing about your relationships, your work, your health, or any of the million and one things you can't control in life, worry manifests in a tornado of panicked thought, fueled by dread and a vivid imagination. And though it may seem imperative and somehow useful to obsess, it doesn't actually accomplish anything. Anxiety puts both your mind and body under immense, prolonged pressure. Your heart races. Your stomach knots up. Your mind feels heavy and overwhelmed. What makes it all the more painful is that you can't always easily trace it to a specific concern. All you know is that everything feels urgent. It's as if something horrible is going to happen, and you have to think your way out of it, and *fast*, or everything will fall apart. And it will all be your fault. At least, this is how it has felt for me.

I first began struggling with anxiety as a young kid, mostly triggered by a fear of not being good enough and a constant sense of impending doom resulting from childhood trauma. That feeling of being unsafe followed me through adolescence and into adulthood, and not just because I was bullied and mistreated, as many of us have been. There came a point when I realized my own mind was a prison, so I couldn't truly feel safe anywhere. No matter where I went, I was controlled by a voice that was as terrified as it was cruel. I needed to do more, to be more, to achieve more, because maybe if I were somehow better than I was, I could insulate myself from life's inevitable pain. Maybe if I were perfect, no one would ever want to hurt me, so I could let my guard down and be happy. And this voice wanted to control not only me, but also the world around me. It liked familiar environments, one-on-one connections with people I trusted, and situations that felt predictable. The unknown was a battlefield surpassed in danger only by my bully brain, which I numbed with food, booze, and cigarettes.

For me, anxiety led to perfectionism, avoidance, self-medicating, and near-constant agonizing about everything that could go wrong. For you, it might lead to other destructive habits, such as codependency or self-harm. Or you might notice subtler unhealthy behaviors, such as fidgeting and obsessive planning for the future. However anxiety and worry impact your life, know that you're far from alone. We're all wired to anticipate and avoid potential threats as a means to keep ourselves safe. And most of us have experienced some form of emotional or physical trauma, resulting in some degree of anxiety, whether acute or debilitating. Perhaps this is why anxiety is the most popular topic on Tiny Buddha: it's pervasive, far more common than you might realize, and it doesn't discriminate, affecting people from all backgrounds and walks of life. For some, it's the pressure to succeed that fuels anxiety. For others, it's a response to abuse or neglect. Life stressors and lifestyle choices can also play a role. Then there's the genetic component, not to mention existential angst—the anxiety we feel when we ponder life, who we are, and the meaning of our existence.

Regardless of what causes us worry and anxiety, both can be crippling. They can suffocate your brain, keep you up at night, and pull you out of the moment. They're the ultimate thieves of time and also the ultimate liars. They can make you doubt yourself, question your choices, and mistrust the people around you. If you're not mindful, you can easily spend your whole life in, or on the verge of, fight-or-flight mode—the physiological reaction that occurs in response to perceived threats. But, as I learned many years ago when I first began my self-help journey, there is another choice. Instead of living life at the mercy of a constantly panicked, catastrophe-predicting mind, we can choose to take a proactive approach to preventing and managing anxiety. We can recognize our triggers, plan ahead to respond to them wisely, and adopt practices that help us develop calm, trust, mindfulness, perspective, and self-acceptance.

The first part of self-acceptance is realizing that the goal isn't to never again worry or panic. Anxiety is a normal human emotion and beneficial in healthy doses. Sometimes threats *aren't* perceived, and our minds serve us well by warning us so that we can stay vigilant. Whether it's a tornado outside your door or a disease you could contract if you don't make healthy choices, there are some things in life that will evoke fear—and that's not only okay, it's crucial. That's not to say *all* anxiety is healthy. If you're feeling persistent, excessive panic that interferes with your ability to function in your daily life, you may require professional help. Though this journal isn't intended to replace that level of care, my hope is that this can be a useful tool to supplement whatever treatment you may receive. It's ideally suited for people like me, who have busy brains and overactive imaginations, and need a little help to become more peaceful and present and less fearful and reactive.

Throughout the journal, you'll find the following:

- Prompts to help you reframe your worries and develop calm, trust, self-acceptance, mindfulness, and perspective
- "Let It Go" pages, all with the same basic template, placed at regular intervals throughout the book, designed to help you work through and release any worries that are weighing you down
- Quotes that may help when you're worrying or feeling anxious, chosen by Tiny Buddha community members
- Coloring pages depicting activities that may help ease anxiety
- Doodle prompts intended to help you draw your way to inner calm
- "Plan Ahead" pages (at the back of the book), which will help you take action to minimize anxiety in your daily life

I chose this mix to offer a wide variety of exercises that may help you foster peace and calm. You'll reap the most benefits if you use this journal regularly, but you don't need to work through each page chronologically. Though it might make sense to fill out all the Plan Ahead pages first, feel free to jump around depending on your mood and your needs. If you're dwelling on the same worries over and over again, turn to a Let It Go page. If you're looking to shift your mind-set and improve your mood, choose one of the pages with prompts, or open to one of the quotation pages and see what that inspires. If you're feeling mentally overwhelmed and need a break from think-ing, color or doodle, and you'll likely find that afterward you feel a lot calmer and more focused. And if ever a prompt or question doesn't feel relevant to you—some may not, since I tried to cover a wide va-riety of topics—feel free to ignore it or write your own. I created a journal that I would want to use, based on what I enjoy and what helps me, but what's most important is that you make this your own and use it however might best help you. It may help to take a few moments to meditate or practice deep breathing before grabbing your pen or marker. Though you certainly don't have to do this, it will likely calm your mind just enough to help you gather your thoughts and find clarity.

I hope this book will be the spark that ignites peace, trust, and calm. I hope it helps you step outside the confines of your fearful, reactive mind and view the world through a wider, clearer lens. Worry and anxiety are part of the human experience, but they don't have to control your life. At any time, you can choose to step back, change your perspective, and let go of what's weighing you down. You just have to choose to do it, one day and one page at a time.

Today, instead of worrying about what could go wrong, I'm going to focus on what could go right, including . . .

_____

_____

_____

_____

_____

_____

_____

_____

_____

_____

_____

_____

_____

_____

_____

_____

_____

Today, I choose to let go of the things I can't control, including . . .

_____

_____

_____

_____

_____

_____

_____

_____

_____

_____

_____

_____

_____

_____

_____

_____

_____

_____

I know it's pointless to worry about what people think of me because . . .

_____

_____

_____

_____

_____

_____

_____

_____

_____

_____

_____

_____

_____

_____

_____

_____

_____

LET IT GO

What's worrying you?

_____

_____

_____

_____

_____

_____

What's not within your control?

_____

_____

_____

_____

_____

_____

What do you need to accept to make peace with those things?

_____

_____

_____

_____

_____

_____

Which of these things are within your control?

_____

_____

_____

_____

_____

What are some solutions you can consider for those things?

_____

_____

_____

_____

_____

What's one simple thing you can do today or tomorrow to begin implementing each solution?

_____

_____

_____

_____

_____

_____

It's not a matter of letting go—you would if you could. Instead of "Let it go," we should probably say "Let it be." ~JON KABAT-ZINN

_____

_____

_____

_____

_____

_____

_____

_____

_____

_____

_____

_____

_____

_____

_____

_____

Imagine that you are putting together a "calm kit" full of physical items that help you stay centered, grounded, and peaceful. Draw below everything you'd carry in this kit, which can be as big as you'd like.

Think about all the expectations you place on yourself and others and the stress and anxiety you feel when these expectations aren't met. Which of these can you let go of today? What's something helpful you can tell yourself when each of these expectations comes to mind?

Expectation: _____

_____

What I'll tell myself: _____

_____

_____

_____

Expectation: _____

_____

What I'll tell myself: _____

_____

_____

_____

Expectation: _____

_____

What I'll tell myself: _____

_____

_____

_____

Write "peace and calm" over and over, filling the page, while breathing deeply.

I recognize that I don't need to have all the answers right now.
Today I give myself permission not to know . . .

_____

_____

_____

_____

_____

_____

_____

_____

_____

_____

_____

_____

_____

_____

_____

_____

LET IT GO

What's worrying you?

_____

_____

_____

_____

_____

_____

What's not within your control?

_____

_____

_____

_____

_____

What do you need to accept to make peace with those things?

_____

_____

_____

_____

_____

Which of these things are within your control?

_____

_____

_____

_____

_____

What are some solutions you can consider for those things?

_____

_____

_____

_____

_____

What's one simple thing you can do today or tomorrow to begin implementing each solution?

_____

_____

_____

_____

_____

_____

Wake up knowing that whatever happens today, you can handle it.
~UNKNOWN

Spend some time near water

I accept that I experience anxiety, and I also accept the following things that I've been resisting . . .

_____

_____

_____

_____

_____

_____

_____

_____

_____

_____

_____

_____

_____

_____

_____

_____

_____

_____

_____

Instead of spending the day caught up in my head, worrying about things that could go wrong, I will be mindful and enjoy the little things, including . . .

_____

_____

_____

_____

_____

_____

_____

_____

_____

_____

_____

_____

_____

_____

It helps me stay calm at work when I . . .

_____

_____

_____

_____

_____

_____

_____

_____

_____

_____

_____

_____

_____

_____

_____

_____

_____

_____

_____

LET IT GO

What's worrying you?

_____

_____

_____

_____

_____

_____

What's not within your control?

_____

_____

_____

_____

_____

_____

What do you need to accept to make peace with those things?

_____

_____

_____

_____

_____

_____

Which of these things are within your control?

_____

_____

_____

_____

_____

What are some solutions you can consider for those things?

_____

_____

_____

_____

_____

What's one simple thing you can do today or tomorrow to begin implementing each solution?

_____

_____

_____

_____

_____

Be gentle with yourself. You're doing the best you can. ~UNKNOWN

Draw a clock (as intricate as you'd like!) and set it to the ideal "worry time" for you—a specific, limited time each day when you'll allow yourself to think about your worries. When you're tempted to worry at another time of day, urge yourself to put that thought aside until your "worry window."

I know I don't need to carry all my responsibilities and burdens on my own, so today I will ask for help with . . .

_____

_____

_____

_____

_____

_____

_____

_____

_____

_____

_____

_____

_____

_____

_____

_____

_____

_____

What's the best advice you ever received about worrying, and how can you apply this today?

_____

_____

_____

_____

_____

_____

_____

_____

_____

_____

_____

_____

_____

_____

_____

_____

_____

Dear inner critic,

You always focus on everything you think I'm doing wrong. But I know I'm doing a lot right, including . . .

_____

_____

_____

_____

_____

_____

_____

_____

_____

_____

_____

_____

_____

_____

_____

LET IT GO

What's worrying you?

_____

_____

_____

_____

_____

_____

What's not within your control?

_____

_____

_____

_____

_____

_____

What do you need to accept to make peace with those things?

_____

_____

_____

_____

_____

_____

Which of these things are within your control?

_____

_____

_____

_____

_____

What are some solutions you can consider for those things?

_____

_____

_____

_____

_____

What's one simple thing you can do today or tomorrow to begin implementing each solution?

_____

_____

_____

_____

_____

Turn your face toward the sun and the shadows will fall behind you.
~MAORI PROVERB

_____

_____

_____

_____

_____

_____

_____

_____

_____

_____

_____

_____

_____

_____

_____

_____

_____

_____

Hug someone
to release
the feel-good
chemical oxytocin

My anxiety does not define me. I am so much more than that.
I am . . .

_____

_____

_____

_____

_____

_____

_____

_____

_____

_____

_____

_____

_____

_____

_____

_____

_____

_____

Today, if I worry that other people are somehow better than I am, I will remember that we are all fundamentally the same. We all . . .

Imagine how your hero or mentor—fictional or real, dead or alive—would handle your current worries, and write the story below.

LET IT GO

What's worrying you?

_____

_____

_____

_____

_____

What's not within your control?

_____

_____

_____

_____

_____

What do you need to accept to make peace with those things?

_____

_____

_____

_____

_____

Which of these things are within your control?

_____

_____

_____

_____

_____

_____

What are some solutions you can consider for those things?

_____

_____

_____

_____

_____

_____

What's one simple thing you can do today or tomorrow to begin
implementing each solution?

_____

_____

_____

_____

_____

_____

May your choices reflect your hopes, not your fears.
~NELSON MANDELA

_____

_____

_____

_____

_____

_____

_____

_____

_____

_____

_____

_____

_____

_____

_____

_____

_____

Draw a series of clouds, then write your worries inside them and imagine them floating away into the sky.

I often worry about my relationship with . . .

_____

_____

_____

_____

_____

I worry about this relationship because . . .

_____

_____

_____

_____

_____

I can calm these worries today by . . .

_____

_____

_____

_____

_____

Write below a list of reasons why it's safe to let go of control.

_____

_____

_____

_____

_____

_____

_____

_____

_____

_____

_____

_____

_____

_____

_____

_____

_____

What are some things you worry about missing out on? Why might it actually be okay to miss out on some things in life?

LET IT GO

What's worrying you?

_____

_____

_____

_____

_____

_____

What's not within your control?

_____

_____

_____

_____

_____

_____

What do you need to accept to make peace with those things?

_____

_____

_____

_____

_____

_____

Which of these things are within your control?

_____

_____

_____

_____

_____

What are some solutions you can consider for those things?

_____

_____

_____

_____

_____

What's one simple thing you can do today or tomorrow to begin
implementing each solution?

_____

_____

_____

_____

_____

_____

No amount of regret can change the past, no amount of worrying can change the future, but any amount of gratitude can change the present. ~UNKNOWN

Get some perspective

Write a letter to yourself from your ninety-year-old self sharing all the reasons why you don't need to worry about what's going on in your life right now.

Dear younger self,

To avoid feeling overwhelmed and anxious, I will prioritize the following things this week:

_____

_____

_____

_____

_____

_____

_____

And I will say no to the following requests:

_____

_____

_____

_____

_____

_____

_____

Imagine a life where there was never anything to worry about because you could control everything that happened. There were never any surprises—nothing to evoke wonder and awe. What would you lose in this scenario?

LET IT GO

What's worrying you?

_____

_____

_____

_____

_____

_____

What's not within your control?

_____

_____

_____

_____

_____

_____

What do you need to accept to make peace with those things?

_____

_____

_____

_____

_____

_____

Which of these things are within your control?

_____

_____

_____

_____

_____

What are some solutions you can consider for those things?

_____

_____

_____

_____

_____

What's one simple thing you can do today or tomorrow to begin implementing each solution?

_____

_____

_____

_____

_____

_____

This too shall pass. It may pass like a kidney stone, but it will pass.
~UNKNOWN

_____

_____

_____

_____

_____

_____

_____

_____

_____

_____

_____

_____

_____

_____

_____

_____

Draw yourself as a superhero—someone totally equipped to handle any challenges that come your way—and list your superpowers next to this drawing.

I know I am strong enough to handle whatever comes at me, because I've survived a lot, including . . .

_____

_____

_____

_____

_____

_____

_____

_____

_____

_____

_____

_____

_____

_____

_____

_____

_____

_____

Since I know it causes anxiety when I attach to specific outcomes, I accept that I can be happy even if the following things don't happen:

Today I will not make people-pleasing choices just to calm my worries about what others think of me.

I will not: _____

_____

_____

_____

_____

_____

_____

_____

Instead, I will: _____

_____

_____

_____

_____

_____

_____

_____

LET IT GO

What's worrying you?

_____

_____

_____

_____

_____

_____

What's not within your control?

_____

_____

_____

_____

_____

_____

What do you need to accept to make peace with those things?

_____

_____

_____

_____

_____

_____

Which of these things are within your control?

_____

_____

_____

_____

_____

What are some solutions you can consider for those things?

_____

_____

_____

_____

_____

What's one simple thing you can do today or tomorrow to begin implementing each solution?

_____

_____

_____

_____

_____

_____

Sometimes the best thing that you can do is not think, not wonder, not imagine, not obsess. Just breathe and have faith that everything will work out for the best. ~UNKNOWN

Make time for meditation

Today I will slow my busy mind by practicing mindfulness in the following activities . . .

Activity: _____

Senses this will engage: _____

What I can enjoy about this activity: _____

_____

_____

_____

Activity: _____

Senses this will engage: _____

What I can enjoy about this activity: _____

_____

_____

_____

Activity: _____

Senses this will engage: _____

What I can enjoy about this activity: _____

_____

_____

_____

I sometimes worry that people may discover the following things about me . . .

_____

_____

_____

_____

_____

_____

_____

_____

I don't need to feel ashamed or worried about these things because . . .

_____

_____

_____

_____

_____

_____

_____

Write below some things you can do to support other people this week, both to help them and to help you get out of your head and stop obsessing about your own worries and problems.

LET IT GO

What's worrying you?

_____

_____

_____

_____

_____

What's not within your control?

_____

_____

_____

_____

What do you need to accept to make peace with those things?

_____

_____

_____

_____

_____

Which of these things are within your control?

_____

_____

_____

_____

_____

What are some solutions you can consider for those things?

_____

_____

_____

_____

_____

What's one simple thing you can do today or tomorrow to begin
implementing each solution?

_____

_____

_____

_____

_____

_____

Between stimulus and response there is a space. In that space is our power to choose our response. In our response lies our growth and our freedom. ~VIKTOR E. FRANKL

Draw a map from your current state of mind to a more peaceful state of mind, and detail all the "stops" (actions/choices) you'll need to make along the way.

Many of the things I've worried about haven't actually happened,
including . . .

_____

_____

_____

_____

_____

_____

_____

_____

_____

_____

_____

_____

_____

_____

_____

_____

Instead of worrying about getting other people's approval, I choose to validate myself. Regardless of what other people think of me, I know that I . . .

Imagine your current struggles are all part of a game, and you receive points for handling your challenges wisely or creatively. What might you get points for doing today?

LET IT GO

What's worrying you?

_____

_____

_____

_____

_____

_____

What's not within your control?

_____

_____

_____

_____

_____

_____

What do you need to accept to make peace with those things?

_____

_____

_____

_____

_____

_____

Which of these things are within your control?

_____

_____

_____

_____

_____

What are some solutions you can consider for those things?

_____

_____

_____

_____

_____

What's one simple thing you can do today or tomorrow to begin implementing each solution?

_____

_____

_____

_____

_____

And you ask, "What if I fall?" Oh, but my darling, what if you fly?
~ERIN HANSON

Prioritize sleep

Write below any beliefs about yourself that cause you anxiety, then list why each belief may not be true.

Belief that causes anxiety: _____

_____

This belief may not be true because: _____

_____

_____

_____

Belief that causes anxiety: _____

_____

This belief may not be true because: _____

_____

_____

_____

Belief that causes anxiety: _____

_____

This belief may not be true because: _____

_____

_____

_____

Instead of worrying about the things I can't control today, I will focus on the things I can control, including . . .

I know I don't always have to worry about other people's problems or pain. I trust that they can handle their problems because . . .

_____

_____

_____

_____

_____

_____

_____

_____

I also know that pain can sometimes be a blessing in disguise because . . .

_____

_____

_____

_____

_____

_____

_____

_____

LET IT GO

What's worrying you?

_____

_____

_____

_____

_____

What's not within your control?

_____

_____

_____

_____

What do you need to accept to make peace with those things?

_____

_____

_____

_____

Which of these things are within your control?

_____

_____

_____

_____

_____

_____

What are some solutions you can consider for those things?

_____

_____

_____

_____

_____

_____

What's one simple thing you can do today or tomorrow to begin implementing each solution?

_____

_____

_____

_____

_____

_____

You can't calm the storm, so stop trying. What you can do is calm yourself. The storm will pass. ~TIMBER HAWKEYE

Draw a large peace sign, and inside the open spaces write any quotes or mantras that bring you peace.

Instead of worrying about making the "wrong" choices, I trust that no matter what I choose . . .

_____

_____

_____

_____

_____

_____

_____

_____

_____

_____

_____

_____

_____

_____

_____

_____

_____

Today, I will not put unnecessary pressure on myself. I accept that things don't need to be perfect, and neither do I. It's good enough to . . .

How could you make today (or tomorrow) easier and less stressful?

_____

_____

_____

_____

_____

_____

_____

_____

_____

_____

_____

_____

_____

_____

_____

_____

_____

_____

LET IT GO

What's worrying you?

_____

_____

_____

_____

_____

What's not within your control?

_____

_____

_____

_____

_____

What do you need to accept to make peace with those things?

_____

_____

_____

_____

_____

Which of these things are within your control?

_____

_____

_____

_____

_____

What are some solutions you can consider for those things?

_____

_____

_____

_____

What's one simple thing you can do today or tomorrow to begin implementing each solution?

_____

_____

_____

_____

_____

So far you've survived 100 percent of your worst days. You're doing great. ~UNKNOWN

Get some exercise

Write about a recent time when anxiety negatively impacted your life, and detail what you learned from that experience that can help you going forward.

The script in my head that is causing anxiety sounds like . . .

_____

_____

_____

_____

_____

_____

I can minimize my anxiety by changing that script to . . .

_____

_____

_____

_____

_____

_____

_____

Picture a peaceful environment that you can visualize in your head whenever you feel anxious, stressed, or overwhelmed. Write below what you see, hear, and smell, and practice visualizing this while taking long, deep breaths.

LET IT GO

What's worrying you?

_____

_____

_____

_____

_____

_____

What's not within your control?

_____

_____

_____

_____

_____

What do you need to accept to make peace with those things?

_____

_____

_____

_____

_____

Which of these things are within your control?

_____

_____

_____

_____

_____

_____

What are some solutions you can consider for those things?

_____

_____

_____

_____

_____

_____

What's one simple thing you can do today or tomorrow to begin
implementing each solution?

_____

_____

_____

_____

_____

_____

Why worry? If you've done the very best you can, worry won't make it any better. ~WALT DISNEY

Draw a newspaper with headlines listing all your recent successes. Refer to this whenever needed as a reminder that you're doing better than you think.

Instead of worrying about all the scary things that are going on in the world, I will do my part, however small, to make the world a better place by . . .

Write below three adjectives to describe how you'd like to be or feel today, and for each, one thing you can do to accomplish that.

I want to feel: _____

_____

_____

One thing I can do to feel this way: _____

_____

_____

I want to feel: _____

_____

_____

One thing I can do to feel this way: _____

_____

_____

I want to feel: _____

_____

_____

One thing I can do to feel this way: _____

_____

_____

Struggling with anxiety doesn't make me a weak person. I know I am strong because . . .

_____

_____

_____

_____

_____

_____

_____

_____

_____

_____

_____

_____

_____

_____

_____

_____

LET IT GO

What's worrying you?

_____

_____

_____

_____

_____

What's not within your control?

_____

_____

_____

_____

_____

What do you need to accept to make peace with those things?

_____

_____

_____

_____

_____

Which of these things are within your control?

_____

_____

_____

_____

_____

What are some solutions you can consider for those things?

_____

_____

_____

_____

_____

What's one simple thing you can do today or tomorrow to begin implementing each solution?

_____

_____

_____

_____

_____

_____

Everything will be okay in the end. If it's not okay, it's not the end.
~JOHN LENNON

Make time for play

The worst thing that could happen is . . .

_____

_____

_____

_____

_____

_____

_____

I could deal with it by . . .

_____

_____

_____

_____

_____

_____

_____

_____

_____

I know it's pointless to worry about things I can't control or change, so instead, today, I will focus on how I respond to those things.

What I can't control or change: _____

_____

_____

How I will respond today: _____

_____

_____

What I can't control or change: _____

_____

_____

How I will respond today: _____

_____

_____

What I can't control or change: _____

_____

_____

How I will respond today: _____

_____

_____

Instead of worrying about other people's opinions of me, I choose to focus on being someone I respect and admire. Today, I will do that by . . .

LET IT GO

What's worrying you?

_____

_____

_____

_____

_____

_____

What's not within your control?

_____

_____

_____

_____

_____

_____

What do you need to accept to make peace with those things?

_____

_____

_____

_____

_____

_____

Which of these things are within your control?

_____

_____

_____

_____

_____

What are some solutions you can consider for those things?

_____

_____

_____

_____

What's one simple thing you can do today or tomorrow to begin implementing each solution?

_____

_____

_____

_____

_____

If you can solve your problem, then what is the need of worrying? If you cannot solve it, then what is the use of worrying? ~SHANTIDEVA

Imagine a recent time when you felt completely at peace and draw the scene below.

Write a letter to your anxiety thanking it for trying to protect you, letting it know how it has negatively affected your life, and explaining why you don't need it so often anymore.

Dear Anxiety,

_____

_____

_____

_____

_____

_____

_____

_____

_____

_____

_____

_____

_____

_____

_____

_____

Think of a day when you experienced minimal or no worry or anxiety. What did you do (or not do) that day? And how can you live more like that day going forward?

List below all the flaws and weaknesses you worry about. Then, next to each, write why it might actually be a strength.

LET IT GO

What's worrying you?

_____

_____

_____

_____

_____

_____

What's not within your control?

_____

_____

_____

_____

_____

What do you need to accept to make peace with those things?

_____

_____

_____

_____

_____

_____

Which of these things are within your control?

_____

_____

_____

_____

_____

_____

What are some solutions you can consider for those things?

_____

_____

_____

_____

_____

What's one simple thing you can do today or tomorrow to begin
implementing each solution?

_____

_____

_____

_____

_____

_____

The best thing about the future is that it comes one day at a time.
~ABRAHAM LINCOLN

_____

_____

_____

_____

_____

_____

_____

_____

_____

_____

_____

_____

_____

_____

_____

_____

_____

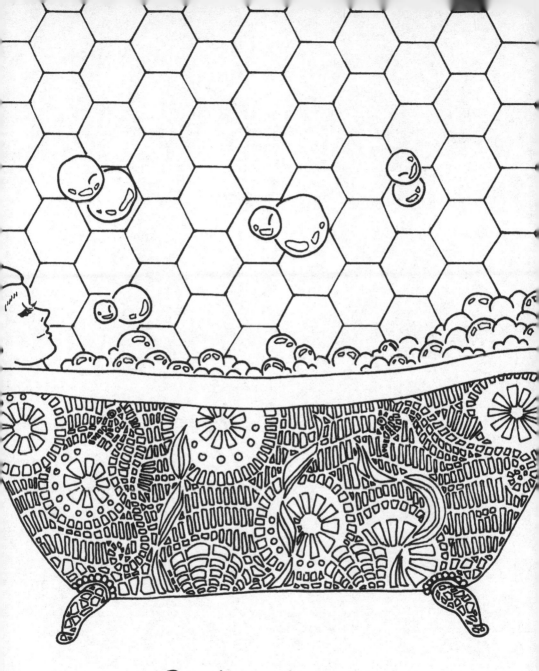

Practice self-care

Instead of thinking anxious thoughts about the future, I choose to focus on how grateful I am for the following things in the present . . .

From here on out I will take care of my own needs without worrying about disappointing or upsetting other people. I give myself permission to . . .

Instead of worrying about what other people are doing (or not doing), today I will be a good role model for others and be the change I wish to see by . . .

_____

_____

_____

_____

_____

_____

_____

_____

_____

_____

_____

_____

_____

_____

_____

_____

_____

LET IT GO

What's worrying you?

_____

_____

_____

_____

_____

What's not within your control?

_____

_____

_____

_____

_____

What do you need to accept to make peace with those things?

_____

_____

_____

_____

_____

Which of these things are within your control?

_____

_____

_____

_____

_____

_____

What are some solutions you can consider for those things?

_____

_____

_____

_____

_____

What's one simple thing you can do today or tomorrow to begin implementing each solution?

_____

_____

_____

_____

_____

_____

Our anxiety does not come from thinking about the future, but from wanting to control it. ~KAHLIL GIBRAN

_____

_____

_____

_____

_____

_____

_____

_____

_____

_____

_____

_____

_____

_____

_____

_____

_____

Draw a staircase with as many steps as you'd like and write on each step one thing you need to do today to feel calm and at peace.

To ease your anxiety about making the "wrong" choices in life, write below your top priorities, in order of importance, as well as your nonnegotiable needs. Refer to this whenever making big decisions so you can trust that you're honoring what's right for you.

I don't need to worry about money, because if my income goes down, I could adapt by . . .

_____

_____

_____

_____

_____

_____

_____

_____

_____

_____

_____

_____

_____

_____

_____

_____

When I feel anxious today, I will repeat the following calming mantras . . .

_____

_____

_____

_____

_____

_____

_____

_____

_____

_____

_____

_____

_____

_____

_____

_____

LET IT GO

What's worrying you?

_____

_____

_____

_____

_____

_____

What's not within your control?

_____

_____

_____

_____

_____

_____

What do you need to accept to make peace with those things?

_____

_____

_____

_____

_____

_____

Which of these things are within your control?

_____

_____

_____

_____

_____

What are some solutions you can consider for those things?

_____

_____

_____

_____

_____

What's one simple thing you can do today or tomorrow to begin implementing each solution?

_____

_____

_____

_____

_____

You don't have to control your thoughts. You just have to stop letting them control you. ~DAN MILLMAN

Strive for balance in life

Anxiety interprets everything negatively. Take a minute to reflect on some of your current worries and how you could interpret those things differently.

Something I'm worried about: _____

_____

_____

A new way to interpret it: _____

_____

_____

Something I'm worried about: _____

_____

_____

A new way to interpret it: _____

_____

_____

Something I'm worried about: _____

_____

_____

A new way to interpret it: _____

_____

_____

If I struggle or worry today, I will treat myself kindly by . . .

_____

_____

_____

_____

_____

_____

_____

_____

_____

_____

_____

_____

_____

_____

It causes me anxiety when I focus my attention on . . .

_____

_____

_____

_____

_____

_____

_____

_____

So instead, today I will focus my attention on . . .

_____

_____

_____

_____

_____

_____

_____

_____

_____

LET IT GO

What's worrying you?

_____

_____

_____

_____

_____

_____

What's not within your control?

_____

_____

_____

_____

_____

What do you need to accept to make peace with those things?

_____

_____

_____

_____

_____

Which of these things are within your control?

_____

_____

_____

_____

_____

What are some solutions you can consider for those things?

_____

_____

_____

_____

_____

What's one simple thing you can do today or tomorrow to begin
implementing each solution?

_____

_____

_____

_____

_____

Worry is a misuse of your imagination. ~DAN ZADRA

_____

_____

_____

_____

_____

_____

_____

_____

_____

_____

_____

_____

_____

_____

_____

_____

_____

_____

Keeping in mind that your inner critic is a scared part of you that just wants to keep you safe, draw him or her below, and give this character a name. In a dialogue bubble, list all the ways it might be trying to protect you. Whenever you feel anxiety stemming from your own harsh internal monologue, visualize this character, send it a silent *thank you*, identify anything helpful it has to say, and consciously choose to let go of anything that doesn't serve you.

Today I will not sweat the small stuff, including . . .

_____

_____

_____

_____

_____

_____

_____

_____

_____

_____

_____

_____

_____

_____

_____

_____

_____

_____

I know that I don't have to face my problems alone because . . .

_____

_____

_____

_____

_____

_____

_____

_____

_____

_____

_____

_____

_____

_____

_____

_____

_____

Write below three things you often worry about losing and how you would rebound if you lost these things.

I worry about losing: _____

_____

_____

I'd be okay if I lost this because: _____

_____

_____

I worry about losing: _____

_____

_____

I'd be okay if I lost this because: _____

_____

_____

I worry about losing: _____

_____

_____

I'd be okay if I lost this because: _____

_____

_____

LET IT GO

What's worrying you?

_____

_____

_____

_____

_____

_____

What's not within your control?

_____

_____

_____

_____

_____

_____

What do you need to accept to make peace with those things?

_____

_____

_____

_____

_____

_____

Which of these things are within your control?

_____

_____

_____

_____

_____

What are some solutions you can consider for those things?

_____

_____

_____

_____

_____

What's one simple thing you can do today or tomorrow to begin implementing each solution?

_____

_____

_____

_____

_____

_____

No feeling is final. ~RAINER MARIA RILKE

Create something with your hands

What's something you've been putting off because you've been worried about the process or the outcome? Write below everything that's been holding you back, what might help you move through those worries, and one thing you can do to get started.

What would you tell a friend if he or she were worrying about the things that have been worrying you?

_____

_____

_____

_____

_____

_____

_____

_____

_____

_____

_____

_____

_____

_____

_____

_____

_____

List below all the "shoulds" and "shouldn'ts" that feed your anxiety (i.e., *I should be perfect; I should have learned this by now*). Then set the intention to let these go today.

LET IT GO

What's worrying you?

_____

_____

_____

_____

_____

What's not within your control?

_____

_____

_____

_____

_____

What do you need to accept to make peace with those things?

_____

_____

_____

_____

_____

Which of these things are within your control?

_____

_____

_____

_____

_____

_____

What are some solutions you can consider for those things?

_____

_____

_____

_____

_____

What's one simple thing you can do today or tomorrow to begin
implementing each solution?

_____

_____

_____

_____

_____

_____

Most things I worry about never happen anyway. ~TOM PETTY

Fill this page with repetitive patterns (i.e., circles of various sizes, wavy lines, or checkered boxes) to get your mind into a state of flow.

Instead of worrying about what I might be missing out on, I will make the most of today by . . .

_____

_____

_____

_____

_____

_____

_____

_____

_____

_____

_____

_____

_____

_____

_____

_____

_____

I will no longer apologize for things that don't require apologies just because I'm worried that other people might be angry or disappointed. I know I don't need to apologize for . . .

Life is more enjoyable when I stop worrying about things I can't control because . . .

_____

_____

_____

_____

_____

_____

_____

_____

_____

_____

_____

_____

_____

_____

_____

_____

LET IT GO

What's worrying you?

_____

_____

_____

_____

_____

What's not within your control?

_____

_____

_____

_____

_____

What do you need to accept to make peace with those things?

_____

_____

_____

_____

_____

Which of these things are within your control?

_____

_____

_____

_____

_____

What are some solutions you can consider for those things?

_____

_____

_____

_____

_____

What's one simple thing you can do today or tomorrow to begin
implementing each solution?

_____

_____

_____

_____

_____

Today is the tomorrow you worried about yesterday.
~DALE CARNEGIE

CHAMOMILE

Try a
natural remedy

Write a script below for a future conversation you've been worried about so you can feel prepared and confident before going into it.

Instead of worrying about my progress or my pace, today I choose to celebrate all I've done and achieved so far. I am proud of myself for . . .

_____

_____

_____

_____

_____

_____

_____

_____

_____

_____

_____

_____

_____

_____

_____

_____

I will no longer be hard on myself for . . .

LET IT GO

What's worrying you?

_____

_____

_____

_____

_____

What's not within your control?

_____

_____

_____

_____

What do you need to accept to make peace with those things?

_____

_____

_____

_____

_____

Which of these things are within your control?

_____

_____

_____

_____

_____

_____

What are some solutions you can consider for those things?

_____

_____

_____

_____

_____

What's one simple thing you can do today or tomorrow to begin implementing each solution?

_____

_____

_____

_____

_____

_____

A problem shared is a problem halved. ~ENGLISH PROVERB

_____

_____

_____

_____

_____

_____

_____

_____

_____

_____

_____

_____

_____

_____

_____

_____

_____

_____

_____

_____

Draw yourself in a beach scene and imagine the sun soothing you and the waves carrying your worries out to sea. If you'd like, write your worries on the waves.

Write below three things you vow to do today to minimize your anxiety and three things you vow not to do.

I vow to:

1. _____

_____

_____

2. _____

_____

_____

3. _____

_____

_____

I vow not to:

1. _____

_____

_____

2. _____

_____

_____

3. _____

_____

_____

Think of a young child in your life, or think back to yourself when you were a kid—before you began carrying the weight of the world on your shoulders. How might you experience this day if you went through it with a sense of childlike presence and innocence, like that kid? What would you do that you don't usually do? What *wouldn't* you do that you usually do?

If I knew today were my last day on Earth, I wouldn't waste time worrying about . . .

_____

_____

_____

_____

_____

_____

_____

_____

_____

_____

_____

_____

_____

_____

_____

_____

_____

LET IT GO

What's worrying you?

_____

_____

_____

_____

_____

_____

What's not within your control?

_____

_____

_____

_____

_____

_____

What do you need to accept to make peace with those things?

_____

_____

_____

_____

_____

_____

Which of these things are within your control?

_____

_____

_____

_____

_____

What are some solutions you can consider for those things?

_____

_____

_____

_____

_____

What's one simple thing you can do today or tomorrow to begin implementing each solution?

_____

_____

_____

_____

_____

You can stand anything for ten seconds. Then you just start on a new ten seconds. ~KIMMY SCHMIDT (FROM *UNBREAKABLE KIMMY SCHMIDT* CREATED BY TINA FEY AND ROBERT CARLOCK)

_____

_____

_____

_____

_____

_____

_____

_____

_____

_____

_____

_____

_____

_____

_____

_____

_____

listen to
calming music

Instead of focusing on getting rid of my anxiety today, I will focus on creating the feeling of _____ by doing the following things:

_____

_____

_____

_____

_____

_____

_____

_____

_____

_____

_____

_____

_____

_____

_____

_____

_____

_____

I know many of the things I'm worrying about today won't matter a year from now, including . . .

_____

_____

_____

_____

_____

_____

_____

_____

_____

_____

_____

_____

_____

_____

_____

_____

_____

_____

Today, if I worry that other people have a better life than I do, I will remind myself of all the things to appreciate about my own life, including . . .

LET IT GO

What's worrying you?

_____

_____

_____

_____

_____

_____

What's not within your control?

_____

_____

_____

_____

_____

What do you need to accept to make peace with those things?

_____

_____

_____

_____

_____

Which of these things are within your control?

_____

_____

_____

_____

_____

_____

What are some solutions you can consider for those things?

_____

_____

_____

_____

_____

What's one simple thing you can do today or tomorrow to begin implementing each solution?

_____

_____

_____

_____

_____

Worry never robs tomorrow of its sorrow, it only saps today of its joy.
~LEO BUSCAGLIA

Write in various letter styles (block letters, bubble letters, cursive, etc.) any words you find calming, and pattern them and/or color them in.

I know uncertainty isn't always a bad thing. Many of the most beautiful moments in my life were completely unexpected, including . . .

If I worry that someone is judging me today, I will remind myself that . . .

_____

_____

_____

_____

_____

_____

_____

_____

_____

_____

_____

_____

_____

_____

_____

_____

_____

_____

Use the space below to challenge the assumptions that are fueling your anxiety.

The facts of the situation I'm worrying about are: _____

_____

_____

_____

_____

_____

My assumptions are: _____

_____

_____

_____

_____

_____

My assumptions may not be true because: _____

_____

_____

_____

_____

_____

LET IT GO

What's worrying you?

_____

_____

_____

_____

_____

_____

What's not within your control?

_____

_____

_____

_____

_____

What do you need to accept to make peace with those things?

_____

_____

_____

_____

_____

_____

Which of these things are within your control?

_____

_____

_____

_____

_____

What are some solutions you can consider for those things?

_____

_____

_____

_____

_____

What's one simple thing you can do today or tomorrow to begin
implementing each solution?

_____

_____

_____

_____

_____

_____

You are exactly where you need to be. ~UNKNOWN

Spend some time with animals

Practice mindfulness right now by writing down everything you can perceive with your senses. Take a few moments to focus solely on these things, then record how you feel after this exercise.

See: _____

_____

Hear: _____

_____

Smell: _____

_____

Feel: _____

_____

Taste: _____

_____

How do you feel now? _____

_____

_____

_____

_____

_____

_____

I would worry a lot less if I let go of . . .

_____

_____

_____

_____

_____

_____

_____

_____

_____

_____

_____

_____

_____

_____

_____

_____

_____

_____

Write below the recipe for a relatively stress-free day. What would it include? What would you need just a dash of or a whole cup of? How can you live this recipe today?

LET IT GO

What's worrying you?

_____

_____

_____

_____

_____

_____

What's not within your control?

_____

_____

_____

_____

_____

_____

What do you need to accept to make peace with those things?

_____

_____

_____

_____

_____

Which of these things are within your control?

_____

_____

_____

_____

_____

What are some solutions you can consider for those things?

_____

_____

_____

_____

_____

What's one simple thing you can do today or tomorrow to begin
implementing each solution?

_____

_____

_____

_____

_____

_____

We would worry less about what others think of us if we realized how seldom they do. ~ETHEL BARRETT

Draw hearts of varying sizes and, in each, write something that fills your heart with peace and joy.

Put on a song that calms you and then write anything that comes to mind. There's no right or wrong way to do this. Vent, give yourself a pep talk, recall a soothing memory—whatever comes up for you.

_____

_____

_____

_____

_____

_____

_____

_____

_____

_____

_____

_____

_____

_____

_____

_____

_____

Today, if I feel overwhelmed with my workload, I will remind myself that . . .

_____

_____

_____

_____

_____

_____

_____

_____

_____

_____

_____

_____

_____

_____

_____

_____

_____

Write below any uncomfortable or painful emotions you're feeling right now and how you know they will eventually pass.

LET IT GO

What's worrying you?

_____

_____

_____

_____

_____

_____

What's not within your control?

_____

_____

_____

_____

_____

_____

What do you need to accept to make peace with those things?

_____

_____

_____

_____

_____

_____

Which of these things are within your control?

_____

_____

_____

_____

_____

What are some solutions you can consider for those things?

_____

_____

_____

_____

_____

What's one simple thing you can do today or tomorrow to begin implementing each solution?

_____

_____

_____

_____

_____

Don't let the behavior of others destroy your inner peace.
~DALAI LAMA

Embrace your imperfect self

Though my anxiety is trying to protect me from harm, I know I am
safe because . . .

_____

_____

_____

_____

_____

_____

_____

_____

_____

_____

_____

_____

_____

_____

_____

_____

_____

_____

Bring to mind a situation you've been worried about and visualize yourself handling it with confidence and ease and coping well if things don't go as you'd hoped. Write below everything you'd think, say, and do in this scenario where you're calm, cool, collected, and capable of handling whatever comes at you.

Write below an encouraging pep talk to help you get through the day, built around the phrase "You got this!"

LET IT GO

What's worrying you?

_____

_____

_____

_____

_____

_____

What's not within your control?

_____

_____

_____

_____

_____

What do you need to accept to make peace with those things?

_____

_____

_____

_____

_____

_____

Which of these things are within your control?

_____

_____

_____

_____

_____

_____

What are some solutions you can consider for those things?

_____

_____

_____

_____

_____

What's one simple thing you can do today or tomorrow to begin implementing each solution?

_____

_____

_____

_____

_____

Never let your fear decide your fate. ~AARON BRUNO

Draw a tree with leaves falling off it. On each leaf, write one thing you need to let go to feel less worried and more peaceful.

Instead of worrying about what could happen in the future, I am going to choose to trust that . . .

_____

_____

_____

_____

_____

_____

_____

_____

_____

_____

_____

_____

_____

_____

_____

_____

_____

_____

If your mind was a library and you were clearing out the books that contribute to your anxiety, what titles would you decide to let go of? Which titles would you replace them with?

_____

_____

_____

_____

_____

_____

_____

_____

_____

_____

_____

_____

_____

_____

_____

_____

List below any aha moments or insights about yourself you had while using this journal.

_____

_____

_____

_____

_____

_____

_____

_____

_____

_____

_____

_____

_____

_____

_____

_____

_____

_____

LET IT GO

What's worrying you?

_____

_____

_____

_____

_____

_____

What's not within your control?

_____

_____

_____

_____

_____

What do you need to accept to make peace with those things?

_____

_____

_____

_____

_____

Which of these things are within your control?

_____

_____

_____

_____

_____

_____

What are some solutions you can consider for those things?

_____

_____

_____

_____

_____

What's one simple thing you can do today or tomorrow to begin implementing each solution?

_____

_____

_____

_____

_____

_____

Don't believe everything you think. ~UNKNOWN

_____

_____

_____

_____

_____

_____

_____

_____

_____

_____

_____

_____

_____

_____

_____

_____

Journal your worries away

PLAN AHEAD QUESTIONS

Create a morning routine to help minimize anxiety at the start of your workday.

What I'll do the night before to make the morning easier: _____

_____

_____

_____

What time I'll wake up: _____

One simple thing I can do for my body: _____

_____

One simple thing I can do for my mind: _____

_____

One simple thing I can do for my spirit: _____

_____

What usually causes me anxiety in the morning, and what I'll do instead: _____

_____

_____

_____

_____

List below people who regularly trigger your anxiety and how you can respond to them differently going forward.

Person who triggers my anxiety: _____

Boundary I can set/how I can respond to them differently: _____

_____

_____

_____

_____

Person who triggers my anxiety: _____

Boundary I can set/how I can respond to them differently: _____

_____

_____

_____

_____

Person who triggers my anxiety: _____

Boundary I can set/how I can respond to them differently: _____

_____

_____

_____

_____

Track your diet for the next week, and list below how often you consume caffeine, alcohol, or high-sugar foods. Then make a plan to minimize your intake and replace these drinks and foods with healthier alternatives.

Alcohol: _____

_____

How I can cut back: _____

_____

_____

Caffeine: _____

_____

How I can cut back: _____

_____

_____

High-sugar foods: _____

_____

How I can cut back: _____

_____

_____

Write below all the ways you enjoy spending time in nature, then schedule some time to do these things in the upcoming weeks to help foster inner peace.

List below all your favorite self-care practices that nurture your mind, body, and spirit. Put some times into your calendar to do these things so you're more likely to stay calm and balanced.

_____

_____

_____

_____

_____

_____

_____

_____

_____

_____

_____

_____

_____

_____

_____

_____

List below your favorite types of exercise—ones that you find enjoyable. When can you fit them into your schedule to help reduce symptoms of anxiety?

_____

_____

_____

_____

_____

_____

_____

_____

_____

_____

_____

_____

_____

_____

_____

_____

_____

Write below any activities that get you into a state of flow and pull you out of your head. Next to each, write when you can fit these activities into your schedule.

Take an inventory of any possessions you can throw away, donate, or organize to create a more calming environment.

I will throw away: _____

_____

_____

_____

_____

_____

I will donate: _____

_____

_____

_____

_____

_____

I will organize: _____

_____

_____

_____

_____

_____

Think about what causes you anxiety and who you can count on to help with these things, then list them below to create an anxiety support plan.

People who will listen without judgment: _____

_____

_____

_____

People who might join for self-care activities: _____

_____

_____

_____

Activities that bring me anxiety and people who can help with each one: _____

_____

_____

_____

Sites or forums to get support: _____

_____

_____

_____

Write below all the ways you can cut back financially, or earn a little extra cash, to help calm worries about money.

I can cancel: _____

_____

_____

I can stop: _____

_____

_____

I can start: _____

_____

_____

I can reduce: _____

_____

_____

I can sell: _____

_____

_____

List below any destructive habits you often turn to when you're anxious, and for each, list something positive and healthy you can do instead.

List below any situations or places you're tempted to avoid because they trigger anxiety, and for each, a mini goal you can set for this week to slowly become more comfortable in this environment. (For example, if you get anxious in crowded places, you can pick up one item in a grocery store that's often crowded.)

_____

_____

_____

_____

_____

_____

_____

_____

_____

_____

_____

_____

_____

_____

_____

_____

List below all the ways technology might trigger worry or anxiety
and some guidelines you can set for yourself to minimize its effects.

Write below any affirmations you can repeat in your mind when you start feeling anxious.

_____

_____

_____

_____

_____

_____

_____

_____

_____

_____

_____

_____

_____

_____

_____

_____

_____

Detail below a calming bedtime ritual to help you get better sleep (which can go a long way in reducing anxiety!). Include things you will do (like read or drink chamomile tea before bed) and things you won't do (like have stressful conversations or look at screens).

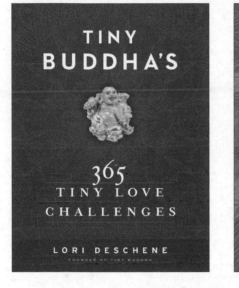
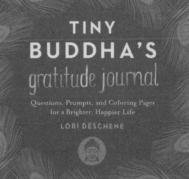